Birds

to Iona
Maiten
Atila

alejando
Lautaro

INTRODUCTION

Bird watching is one of our most popular pastimes and it is easy to see why. By some estimates there are more than 11 000 different kinds of birds that have been identified throughout the world. Britain alone can boast a list of more than 400 species. The RSPB (Royal Society for the Protection of Birds) does a great job in identifying species at risk in the UK and protecting them to increase their numbers. They operate a priority listing, with their 'Red List' showing those birds most at risk.

Although the basic body shape of all birds remains the same, there is a wide variety of sizes. Wings and tails come in different shapes and sizes, as do legs and beaks. These variations reflect the kind of habitat in which the bird lives as well as the type of food it eats and other aspects of its behaviour. The colours of birds' feathers can also reflect the habitat they live in and whether or not they need to be camouflaged from predators. Colours can vary greatly, not just between species but also between the males and females of the same species. Young birds – known as juveniles – are usually different colours from the adult birds, and some birds change their colours with the seasons too!

Birds' songs are often a joy to listen to as they claim their territories in spring. Every song is different and with patience, it is possible to identify many birds without seeing them at all.

You do not even need to stray from your house and garden to enjoy watching the antics of tits at a bag of nuts, house sparrows dust bathing or blackbirds tugging away at a resistant worm in the lawn. Finally, by setting out the right kinds of food and water, it is possible to attract many different sorts of birds to your garden so that in a way, your garden becomes an 'unofficial' bird reserve.

How to use your i-SPY book

The birds in this book are arranged in much the same way as in most identification guides. In most cases, the male birds are illustrated, as females are often more drably coloured. You need 1000 points to send off for your i-SPY certificate (see page 64) but that is not too difficult because there are masses of points in every book. Each entry has a star or circle and points value beside it. The stars represent harder to spot entries. As you make each i-SPY, write your score in the circle or star. For entries where there is a question, double your score if you can answer it. Answers are shown on page 63.

CANADA GOOSE

Points: 10

As their name suggests, these well-known geese originally came from North America but they were introduced into Europe more than 200 years ago. You can see them on lakes and ponds or in fields.

Points: 5
double with answer

MALLARD

Everyone knows the Mallard. It is the bird that you always think of as a typical wild duck.

Ducks and drakes look identical. True or False?

3

Points: 20

MANDARIN DUCK

Originally from China, this beautiful bird has, thankfully, escaped from private collections of ornamental wildfowl and now adorns our lakes and slower rivers. Unusually for a duck, it nests in holes in trees.

POCHARD

Points: 25

The Pochard is a striking bird that regularly visits the ponds and lakes in London's Royal Parks. However, its preferred home is flooded gravel pits and other large lakes.

Points: 10

DUNNOCK

Often seen around hedges and wrongly called the Hedge Sparrow, it is not related to sparrows. The two birds have different beak shapes and different food requirements. They are often seen quietly and efficiently picking up scraps under the bird table.

WREN

Points: 15

This is a tiny bird and, although it is very common, its habit of hiding in hedges and holes in banks makes it hard to see. Its Latin name of Troglodytes means 'cavedweller'. For such a small bird, it has a very loud song.

Points: 10

STARLING

One of the Starling's most noticeable characteristics is that in winter, in certain places, roosting flocks of millions are a daily spectacle! Also, it's an excellent mimic – phones and alarms are a speciality!

LONG-TAILED TIT

Points: 10

With its plump little body and long tail, this delightful member of the tit family is easy to recognise. It is found in woodland and hedgerows.

Points: 15

HOUSE SPARROW

Everyone can recognise this little bird because it is found so close to houses and farms. It will readily feed on household scraps and seeds from the bird table as well as on insects.

COAL TIT

Points: 15

The Coal Tit has a black cap with a white patch in it. These birds are usually found in mixed woodlands, and in winter they join mixed-species flocks to visit bird tables and feeders.

 Points: 5

BLUE TIT

A popular garden visitor, these little birds are familiar because of their acrobatics at bird feeders. A gardener's friend, they eat more aphids (small plant-eating insects) than any other species.

GREAT TIT

Points: 5

With its blue-black head, white cheek patches, and yellow breast with a black bar down the centre, this is an easy bird to identify. The male's 'teacher teacher' song is also a familiar spring sound.

Points: 15

SWIFT

With their long, sickle-shaped wings and fast, agile flight, these birds are well named. Listen for their shrill scream – made at breakneck speed just feet above the ground or high in the sky. Swifts have been known to stay aloft for more than 100 days without landing.

HOUSE MARTIN

Points: 15
double with answer

It is the white bar at the base of the tail which will allow you to distinguish these birds from Swallows or Swifts.

When they do not nest on houses, where would you expect them to build their nests?

PIED WAGTAIL

Points: 5

The Pied Wagtail is black and white and its plumage makes this bird hard to miss. It's always rushing about flicking its tail while searching for insects. It's not just a countryside bird and it often roosts in large numbers in cities.

Points: 5
double with answer

ROBIN

Some books suggest that it is only the male Robin which has the familiar red breast. This is quite untrue and the sexes are almost impossible to tell apart.

Robins have an autumn/winter song and a spring/summer song.
True or False?

BLACKBIRD

Points: 5

With his shiny black plumage, yellow beak, and yellow ring round his eye, the male Blackbird is a handsome bird. His song is also very musical. The female is a dark brown colour.

Points: 5

CHAFFINCH

This is a very familiar bird, and the male's colours of bluish-grey, pink, brown, black and white make it stand out. The female has roughly the same pattern but the colours are duller.

GREENFINCH

Points: 10

The male bird is a bright yellowish green while the female is rather duller. Look for these birds in woodland, along hedgerows, in parks, and even in your garden.

Points: 10

GOLDFINCH

The bright red, white, black, and yellow colours of this delightful little finch make it easy to recognise. It is often seen feeding on the seeds of thistle heads in autumn.

Points: 30

BRAMBLING

More than a million of these colourful finches arrive in the UK in late September. They are about the same size as a Chaffinch, with whom they often form large flocks.

GREAT CRESTED GREBE

Points: 15

This attractive bird breeds on lakes, flooded gravel pits and sometimes on rivers. Look out for the head tufts during the breeding season.

Points: 10

MOORHEN

Moorhens are found in most kinds of watery areas where there are plants growing. Sometimes they may be quite shy. Look out for the red area on the front of the head and base of the beak as well as the constantly flicking white tail.

COOT

Points: 10

'As bald as a Coot!' or so the saying goes. Coots are not actually bald but they do have a white patch on the forehead and beak. They are found on lakes, flooded gravel pits and reservoirs.

Points: 30

PINTAIL

Larger than a Mallard, its pointed wings and tapering tail make it easy to distinguish from other ducks. They live in marshy ground while breeding and move to estuaries during winter to join the many thousands that migrate from Europe.

GOLDENEYE

Points: 25

Spotting a Goldeneye is getting easier; they are now quite common in winter around inland waterways and marshes. Rather unusually for ducks, they nest in trees and are being encouraged to nest in special nestboxes so that we have them here all year round.

Points: 10

TUFTED DUCK

This black and white duck gets its name from the tuft on its head. They can be found in great numbers on lakes, reservoirs and flooded gravel pits.

SHOVELER

Points: 30

An unmistakable duck, its wide, flat specialised bill enables it to filter feed on weeds, crustaceans and small insects at the water's edge. It prefers areas of deep cover, and outside of the breeding season, even the drake (male) is actually quite drab. The best place to see a Shoveler would be a nature reserve during winter.

TEAL

Points: 20

The Teal is our smallest duck. They are never far from water and nest in thick vegetation beside bogs and pools on northern moorland. During winter they form large flocks and gather to feed on estuaries and adjacent grassland.

 Points: 20

REED WARBLER

This summer migrant is a small brownish bird with a paler underside. The delicate-looking bill is quite long. They nest only in reed beds and are a major host for the Cuckoo. Listen for the chattering song.

SEDGE WARBLER

Points: 15

This warbler is a widely seen summer visitor from Africa. It's not shy or quiet and can often be spotted singing its random song from a bush at the edge of a reedbed. It can be distinguished from other warblers by the creamy stripe above its eye.

Points: 40   Top Spot!

REED BUNTING

This bird lives in wetlands and nests in plants along the water's edge. In the breeding season, it is often to be seen at the top of a reed or bulrush stem, singing loudly. It feeds on both seeds and insects.

GREY HERON

Points: 15

The Grey Heron is easy to recognise even in flight. It flies with slow, lazy-looking wing beats and its long legs trail out behind. It is often mobbed by smaller birds.

Points: 5
double with answer

BLACK-HEADED GULL

These common gulls are not only seen at the coast. During the winter, you can see them in most areas

Look carefully, what colour are their heads in winter?

Points: 40   Top Spot!

ARCTIC TERN

The Arctic Tern and the Common Tern are quite hard to tell apart so birdwatchers often group them together under the name 'Comic Tern'. Look out for their bouncing flight and forked tails.

COMMON TERN

Points: 15

Nicknamed the 'sea swallow', these graceful birds frequently hover over water before plunging down for a fish.

Points: 25

BRENT GOOSE

This goose is about the size of a large duck. They are usually seen around coastal mudflats where they feed mainly on eel grass during the winter. They are winter visitors to the UK, escaping the cold of Russia and Greenland.

SHELDUCK

Points: 15

The bold colours of this bird make it easily recognisable even at a distance. It is usually found around coastal estuaries. Look out for the red knob at the base of the male's beak.

Points: 5
double with answer

MUTE SWAN

This bird is quite unmistakable. It has been said that it is the heaviest bird capable of flying long distances.

Male and female are often given special names – what are they?

Points: 10

GREYLAG GOOSE

The Greylag is the largest and bulkiest of the wild geese native to the UK. With its pink legs, a large head and an almost triangular orange-pink bill it's easy to identify.

OYSTERCATCHER

Points: 10

With its bright red bill, red legs, red eyes and black and white plumage, the Oystercatcher is easy to recognise at the coast. Listen for its loud piping call.

Points: 15

RINGED PLOVER

In the winter, these attractive little shore birds are found along muddy estuaries. For the rest of the year, look for them along sandy or shingly coasts.

DUNLIN

Points: 15

These little birds are common shore birds and may be seen in large flocks. You can see them dashing about the mud probing for food with their beaks.

 Points: 15

REDSHANK

This is another common wading bird and, as its name suggests, it has red legs as well as a reddish base to its bill. They feed on estuaries during the winter.

COMMON SANDPIPER

Points: 15

With its white underside, brownish back, and its habit of bobbing up and down when it is on the ground, this bird is quite easy to recognise.

Points: 20

KINGFISHER

Although these birds have a striking, orange-coloured breast, when you see them in flight they look like small electric-blue arrows. They hunt small fish and invertebrates from riverside perches and nest at the end of tunnels that they dig in vertical banks.

DIPPER

Top Spot!   **Points: 40**

The Dipper is a small brown bird with a white breast; it lives by fast-flowing streams and shallow, swift rivers. It bobs up and down on the bank prior to walking into the water where it uses its wings and sharp claws to stabilise itself while hunting insect larvae on the river bed.

Points: 50   Top Spot!

BEWICK'S SWAN

These are our smallest swans but they undertake an epic journey, travelling thousands of miles from Siberia to spend the winter here.

Points: 50   Top Spot!

AVOCET

This bird was almost extinct in the UK but conservation action brought it back from a few pairs in 1940 to over 1500 today. It eats aquatic insects and larvae using its specialised bill.

Points: 20

SAND MARTIN

In general shape, this bird looks like a House Martin but it is brown in colour above and has a white underside with a brown bar across its chest. It nests in burrows in sandy cliffs.

LITTLE GREBE

Points: 25

Another bird which delights in man-made lakes and waterways, they are often seen on quiet parts of canal systems. If alarmed they will dive and emerge a fair distance from the perceived danger.

Points: 20

GREY WAGTAIL

Grey Wagtails have conspicuous yellow patches on their breasts and rumps. They are found by fast-flowing streams and often nest under bridges.

WHITE-FRONTED GOOSE

Points: 30

It is unusual in that two distinct populations visit the British Isles but only between October and March and they do not breed. The name refers to the white patch on the front of the face.

Points: 25

TURNSTONE

A small but sturdy bird that spends its time doing what its name says – turning over stones using its strong bill to search for a meal. Notice the bright orange-red legs.

WIGEON

Points: 25

These are easily located by their unmistakable whistling call. Flocks of thousands can be readily seen in winter as residents are supplemented by migrants from Russia and the East.

Points: 20

CORMORANT

These large birds nest on sea cliffs but they may be seen quite far inland on rivers. Watch out for them holding out their wings to dry after they have been diving for food.

SHAG

Points: 15

The Shag is smaller than the Cormorant and is rarely seen away from the coast. In the spring the bird boasts a crest on its head. The plumage appears dark green and oily.

HERRING GULL

Points: 10

The Herring Gull is a large, heavily built bird with pink legs and a yellow bill bearing a bright red spot on the underside. It is found mainly at the coast, but also on rubbish tips.

 Points: 15

GREAT BLACK-BACKED GULL

The Great Black-backed Gull is even bigger and more powerful than the Herring Gull. It will even attack other birds, especially their chicks in the breeding season. Usually a solitary bird, it may also be seen in mixed gull flocks.

Points: 25

KITTIWAKE

This medium-sized gull is noted for its black wing-tips. The Kittiwake is a strictly coastal gull and spends the winter months out at sea.

PUFFIN

Points: 25

The Puffin is recognised by everybody. In March they arrive at their traditional breeding colonies on the coast where they nest in tunnels. They leave in August to spend the winter far out to sea.

Points: 20

RAZORBILL

It is not always easy to tell Guillemots and Razorbills apart unless they are in mixed colonies, when this bird looks blacker and rather bigger than the Guillemot.

COMMON GULL

Points: 5

A smaller version of the Herring Gull, it is abundant in coastal regions and in some eastern counties. They are often seen in towns and on housing estates in winter.

 Points: 20

FULMAR

This grey and white seabird only comes to land to breed. It is present around its breeding sites for most of the year where it glides low over the sea looking for a meal. It mostly feeds on waste fish from trawlers.

GUILLEMOT

Points: 20

When they sit upon rocks at the coast, these members of the auk family resemble Penguins. They nest on bare ledges on sea cliffs. They are fast fliers and good swimmers.

Points: 30

EIDER DUCK

The Eider is a true seaduck, rarely found inland. They nest on the ground, usually on small islands for safety. Until quite recently, their old down-lined nests were collected, cleaned and used in quilts. The male and female are very different.

GANNET

Points: 25

The Gannet is our largest seabird with a wingspan of up to 180 cm (71 inches)! These birds dive for fish and are shaped like arrows – everything is streamlined and designed to pierce the water. They nest in huge numbers on steep cliffs but can often be seen from the shore.

Points: 50   **Top Spot!**

PEREGRINE

This fast-flying, anchor-shaped falcon feeds mainly on birds such as pigeons and doves, which it catches in flight. It swoops down on its victim and is the fastest creature in the world.

HEN HARRIER

Points: 30

This is the female, drab in comparison to the male who has beautiful blue-grey plumage and a white belly with a yellow eye, making him very distinctive. They tend to breed on moorlands and at other times can be found gliding slowly over coastal fields and marshes.

Points: 40   **Top Spot!**

MERLIN

This falcon is smaller and faster than a Kestrel. It hunts down small moorland birds like larks and pipits which it spots from shrubs, stunted trees, and sometimes fenceposts. During the winter it frequents our coastal grasslands where it preys on winter migrants.

CURLEW

Points: 25

This is our largest wader. It nests on moorlands and spends the rest of the year at the coast where it uses its long, curved bill to probe in the mud for worms and shrimps. Its name comes from its 'cooer- leeoo' call.

Points: 15

STOCK DOVE

Stock Doves are found in farmland, parks, the edges of woods, cliffs, ruined buildings and even among sand dunes. Unlike Woodpigeons they nest in holes and feed mainly on seeds.

HOODED CROW

Points: 15

Unlike Carrion Crows, 'Hoodies' often gather in flocks. They have adapted to a harsh life and are omnivorous, feeding on carrion when it's available.

Points: 40   **Top Spot!**

SHORT-EARED OWL

Short-eared Owls are found in open country such as moorland. The word 'ear' refers to tufts of feathers on the head of the bird, though these aren't actually the owl's ears.

SNIPE

Points: 25

This long-billed bird is best known for its habit of 'drumming' during the breeding season. It flies up and then dives with its outer tail feathers spread out to make a throbbing noise.

Points: 50   Top Spot!

DOTTEREL

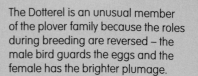

The Dotterel is an unusual member of the plover family because the roles during breeding are reversed – the male bird guards the eggs and the female has the brighter plumage.

GOLDEN PLOVER

Points: 20

This is a medium-sized plover with an upstanding posture and amazing gold and black summer plumage. In winter they gather in great numbers and fly about in formation. During the summer they are breeding on moorlands but move to lowland fields to overwinter.

Points: 35
double with answer

Top Spot!

GOLDEN EAGLE

The sheer size of this bird is usually enough to give it away. It has broad wings with 'fingered' tips on which it soars while looking for live prey, like mountain hares, and carrion.

It is estimated that around 400 pairs live in Scotland, with a few visiting Northern England each year looking for new territories to expand into.

How does the bird get its name?

RAVEN

Points: 30

The Raven is the largest member of the crow family, and is even larger than a Buzzard! It is completely black with a large bill and a diamond-shaped tail.

Points: 15

MEADOW PIPIT

This small brown bird has a longish tail which it flicks as it runs along the ground. It is usually found in open grassland or moorland.

Points: 20

The Tree Pipit sings as it flies from perch to perch. It resembles a small thrush covered in brown streaks even on its back; it has pink legs and a pale stripe above the eye. It's a common summer visitor and populates our heath, moorland and young tree plantations, eating small insects and berries.

STONECHAT

Points: 15

This black, white and orange bird is found on heaths, commons and moors. It gets its name from its call which sounds like two pebbles being knocked together.

37

WHEATEAR

Points: 15 15

The male Wheatear has a grey back, white rump, black face stripes and orange-pink chest; the female (shown here) is paler and lacks the black cheeks. These birds are summer migrants from Africa and are commonly found on open moorland.

15 **Points: 15**

RED GROUSE

Also called the Willow Grouse though they are always found on heather moorland. When disturbed, they fly low with a call which sounds like 'Go back. Go back.'

BLACK GROUSE

Top Spot! **Points: 50**

The male and female, both with a distinctive lyre-shaped tail, are often called 'Black Cock' and 'Grey Hen'. They are rare even on their upland moorland habitat, and are very sensitive to disturbance.

Points: 50 **Top Spot!**

PTARMIGAN

If you are lucky enough to see a male Ptarmigan in winter, it is likely to have changed its plumage from dark brown to all white. They are found on heather moors in Scotland.

BUZZARD

Points: 25

Conservationists have triumphed! Buzzards can once again regularly be seen wheeling over all kinds of open country either singly or in small family groups after their numbers had fallen. Listen for their 'mewing' call.

Points: 25

SPARROWHAWK

Look for the Sparrowhawk as it dashes along and over hedgerows – it's trying to catch small birds by surprise. The female Sparrowhawk is larger and browner than the male.

Points: 5

KESTREL

It is easy to see why this bird gets its country name of 'Windhover'. Look out for them hovering by roads and motorways searching for insects and small mammals to pounce on.

LAPWING

Points: 30
double with answer

Flocks of Lapwings can be seen feeding on pasture and ploughed fields. They need undisturbed fields, such as meadows, set-aside for nesting. Although their upper parts are greenish, in flight they look black and white.

Can you think of two other common names for this bird?

Points: 15

MARSH TIT

The Marsh Tit and Willow Tit look very similar with their black caps and, despite their names, both birds live in woodland. However, it is the Willow Tit that likes to be near water.

Points: 25

SPOTTED FLYCATCHER

Spotted Flycatchers arrive here in May and stay until August. While here they happily nest in farmyards, large gardens or open woodland. They feed by perching on tall shrubs or roofs watching for passing insects. Recent cold, wet summers have not helped their population.

BARN OWL

Top Spot!   Points: 40

40

This is a long-winged, night hunting bird. Its breast may be near white or rather more golden and sometimes the bird almost seems to glow in the dark. They do not hoot but screech and hiss.

LITTLE OWL

Points: 25

You may see Little Owls during the day sitting on a fence post looking for insects. As its name suggests, it is a small owl, at just 22 cm (8.5 inches) in height.

Points: 30
double with answer

GREEN WOODPECKER

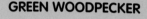

This brightly coloured, greenish-yellow woodpecker may even be seen in gardens. It is sometimes called the 'Yaffle' because of its laughing song.

What is very noticeable about this bird's flight?

GREAT SPOTTED WOODPECKER

Points: 15

This black and white woodpecker has a red patch beneath its tail. It 'sings' by drumming its beak against a trunk or branch of a tree. The bird feeds on insects which it digs out from under the bark.

SKYLARK

Points: 20

As the male bird climbs into the air on rapidly beating wings, it produces its loud, warbling song. This song is a familiar sound of summer in open countryside and farmland.

Points: 15

SWALLOW

Familar birds of summer, Swallows feed by catching insects in flight. They will also swoop down over lakes and rivers to drink. Look out for their long tail streamers.

YELLOW WAGTAIL

Points: 20

Yellow Wagtails are found in damp fields and water meadows, flooded gravel pits, wet moorland and farmland near water. They feed on insects and other small creatures.

Points: 20

SONG THRUSH

Song Thrushes are found in gardens, woods and hedgerows. The brown back and speckled breast make this an easy bird to identify.

MISTLE THRUSH

Points: 10

This is our largest thrush. It can be aggressive and will drive off birds like Magpies from its territory if required. It's easy to spot singing from the top of a tall tree; its plumage is slightly greyer than that of the Song Thrush.

Points: 15

FIELDFARE

Its large size, grey head and rump, and darker end to the tail make this thrush easy to recognise. These birds breed in open woodland but gather in large flocks on farmland from October to March.

REDWING

Points: 15

Redwings are the smallest members of the thrush family. Large flocks inhabit open fields, eating worms and also berries from the hedgerow. They aren't too hard to see as almost 750 000 birds arrive in the UK to overwinter until March.

Points: 15

CHIFFCHAFF

The Chiffchaff is a summer migrant that looks very like the Willow Warbler except that it has dark-coloured legs. But it gets its name from its song – a repetitive 'chiff-chaff, chiff-chaff'.

BLACKCAP

Points: 15

A handsome warbler with a beautiful song that lifts the spirits when it returns to us in spring from Northern Europe. A few spend the winter here and become regular visitors to the garden and bird table. They spend a large part of their lives in thick cover but the singing of the male gives them away. The female is similar but with a brown cap.

Points: 15

WHITETHROAT

With its brownish body, greyer head and distinctive white throat, this summer migrant is one of the easier warblers to recognise. It is found in woodlands and shrubbery.

Points: 30

BULLFINCH

An unmistakable British bird now on the RSPB Red List due to habitat decline and modern pesticides used by farmers. This gloriously pinkie-red male and his duller female were once common and a well known pest in fruit orchards where they devoured buds, seeds and insects.

SISKIN

Points: 15

The Siskin looks rather like a Greenfinch, except that the male Siskin has a black crown and chin and rather more yellow colours on the underside. These birds eat the seeds of cones.

Points: 15

LINNET

These birds are greyish brown above and paler on the underside but, in spring and summer, the chest of the male bird is flushed with pink. They are found in open country where there are trees and bushes.

YELLOWHAMMER

Points: 10
double with answer

It is the bright yellow head of the male bird which is easy to spot. Listen to his song in spring and summer, as he sits atop a hedge or gate post.

What does he seem to say?

CORN BUNTING

Points: 10

This bird is rather similar to the Yellowhammer but it lacks the bright yellow colours. Its song sounds like the rattling of a bunch of keys after a 'chinkchink' start.

Points: 5

MAGPIE

With its very long tail and bold black and white colours, this is an easy bird to recognise. You will often see them at the roadside feeding on animals that were killed on the roads.

ROOK

Points: 5

This is a large, glossy black bird with a long bill that has a grey base. It is often found in large flocks feeding on open farmland or in parks and gardens.

Points: 15

CARRION CROW

This clever member of the crow family is completely black, including its stout bill that can be used to carry large objects. It is usually solitary but may be found in small family parties.

WOODPIGEON

Points: 5

When Woodpigeons take off, they usually make a loud clapping noise with their wings as they strike together. This is thought to help them make a fast getaway.

COLLARED DOVE

Points: 5

With their pinkish, fawnish, grey colour and black, collar-like mark on either side of the neck, these birds are easy to recognise. They can often be seen in gardens.

Points: 15

RED-LEGGED PARTRIDGE

Nicknamed 'Frenchmen' by the shooting fraternity, this type of partridge has been introduced into Britain from mainland Europe. It is slightly larger than our native breed and appears to thrive in farmland bounded by woods.

PHEASANT

Points: 10

The brightly coloured male Pheasant is unmistakable. These birds are found in most types of country where there are seeds and berries to feed on.

Points: 30

GREY PARTRIDGE

An orange-faced, plump-breasted gamebird that has joined the RSPB Red List due to habitat loss and modern farming methods. They are sociable birds outside of the breeding season and form into groups called 'coveys' for safety.

QUAIL

Top Spot! **Points: 50**

At 18 cm (7 inches), this diminutive gamebird comes to visit us in the late spring and stays until autumn. It hunts for insects in standing crops.

GOSHAWK

Top Spot! **Points: 50**

It's almost as large as a Buzzard but this handsome hawk is more agile. It often hunts birds up to Pigeon size by chasing them through the trees at high speed but will also soar in order to spot mammals and birds on the ground. As usual with birds of prey, the female is larger than the male.

Points: 30

TREECREEPER

A secretive, small, brown speckled bird which feeds on bugs hiding in the bark of trees, though not much can hide from that thin, curved beak. It spirals up to the top of the tree then flies to the bottom of the next one to start climbing and feeding all over again.

Points: 25

LESSER SPOTTED WOODPECKER

This is like a smaller version of the Great Spotted; the male bird has a red cap. The drumming song is quieter and more rapid than that of its larger cousin.

NUTHATCH

Points: 20

The Nuthatch will readily visit garden feeders. In the wild woodland it scrambles around on tree trunks and branches looking for insects.

Points: 25

CUCKOO

The Cuckoo is more often heard than seen; they are sometimes mistaken for birds of prey in flight. They are best known for their habit of laying their eggs in the nests of other birds.

GOLDCREST

Points: 30

This is a tiny, greenish-coloured bird that is usually seen flitting from branch to branch on larches and other coniferous trees. If you see one, look for the yellow stripe with black lines on either side on the bird's head.

Points: 15

JAY

This brightly coloured member of the crow family is usually a shy bird and you are lucky if you see one flying between patches of woodland. Sometimes, though, they do turn up in gardens.

JACKDAW

Points: 5

Smaller than a Rook or a Crow and with a greyish head and rather untidy appearance, the Jackdaw is quite easy to identify. Its harsh 'keeaw' call is also very noticeable.

Points: 40   Top Spot!

TAWNY OWL

This is the woodland owl which makes the familiar hooting noise. If you see mobs of small birds seemingly attacking an ivy-covered tree, there may well be a Tawny Owl roosting there.

TURTLE DOVE

Points: 25

The Turtle Dove is a summer visitor from Africa, usually found in open woodland in the southeast of England. They are more often heard than seen, and make a pleasant purring sound.

LITTLE EGRET

Points: 25

Only 10 years ago it was rare to see a Little Egret. It is now commonly sighted in marshes and rivers, but most often in large numbers at favoured coastal sites.

Points: 50   **Top Spot!**

BITTERN

The brown and black Bitterns usually frequent reedbeds and similar marshy areas, feeding on amphibians, reptiles, insects and fish. The male has a distinctive low-pitched mating call - a far carrying 'boom'.

Points: 25

This reddy coloured bird of prey is quite easily recognised from its 'floating' flight, 165 cm (65 inch) wingspan and forked tail. Since the 1980s it has been brought back from national extinction and in some areas can be seen in small flocks.

Points: 50   Top Spot!

OSPREY

Ospreys are rare summer visitors to very specific locations in Scotland, England and Wales. These are the sanctuaries where, with luck, the birds will nest and a good view can be had. They feed by swooping down and grasping a fish from the water.

HOOPOE

Top Spot!   Points: 50

With its curved bill, black and white wings, bright pinkish plumage and large crest, this foreign visitor is very distinctive. It occasionally arrives along the south coast by mistake! So far it has not nested here but with Britain's climate change, who knows?

Points: 20

RING-NECKED PARAKEET

These handsome parrots were introduced to southeast England in the early 1970s and have now increased to many thousands thanks to abundant bird table offerings and garden fruit.

Points: 50 **Top Spot!**

GREAT BUSTARD

Persecuted to local extinction in the 1840s, the Bustard is on the way back thanks to a well-guarded conservation project which, since 2004 has released over 50 individually tagged adult birds on to Salisbury Plain. The first chicks were raised in 2009.

WAXWING

Top Spot! **Points: 50**

The Waxwing visits when winter food supplies dwindle in its regular home territory of Scandinavia. It comes here for berries and fruit such as hawthorn and rowan.

INDEX

Answers: P3 False. **P8** Cliffs and caves. **P9** True. **P17** White with faint vertical streaks. **P19** Male = Cob, Female = Pen. **P35** Its neck and head are gold in colour. **P41** Peewit and Green Plover. **P44** It swoops along like the big dipper at the funfair. **P50** Little bit of bread and no cheese'.

i-SPY

How to get your i-SPY certificate and badge

Let us know when you've become a super-spotter with 1000 points and we'll send you a special certificate and badge!

HERE'S WHAT TO DO!

- ✓ Ask an adult to check your score.

- ✓ Visit www.collins.co.uk/i-SPY to apply for your certificate. If you are under the age of 13 you will need a parent or guardian to do this.

- ✓ We'll send your certificate via email and you'll receive a brilliant badge through the post!